GORILLAS

by Andrea Wang

Content Consultant
Alison A. Elgart, PhD
Associate Professor, Anthropology Program
Florida Gulf Coast University

CORE
LIBRARY

Printed in the United States of America,
North Mankato, Minnesota
092013
012014

♻ THIS BOOK CONTAINS AT LEAST 10% RECYCLED MATERIALS.

Editor: Mirella Miller
Series Designer: Becky Daum

Library of Congress Cataloging-in-Publication Data
Wang, Andrea.
  Gorillas / by Andrea Wang.
    pages cm. -- (The smartest animals)
  Includes bibliographical references and index.
  ISBN 978-1-62403-168-7
1. Gorilla--Juvenile literature. I. Title.
  QL737.P96W365 2014
  599.884--dc23
                    2013029173

Photo Credits: Mike Price/Shutterstock Images, cover, 1; Erik Zandboer/ Shutterstock Images, 4; iStockphoto/Thinkstock, 7, 9, 36, 43; Elzbieta Sekowska/Shutterstock Images, 7; Shutterstock Images, 7, 11; Minden Pictures/SuperStock, 12, 39; Vidiphoto/Picture-Alliance/DPA/AP Images, 15; NaturePL/SuperStock, 17; Yair Leibovich/Shutterstock Images, 20; Thomas Breuer/Wildlife Conservation Society/AP Images, 23, 45; Bettmann/Corbis/AP Images, 26; Sergey Uryadnikov/Shutterstock Images, 28; Red Line Editorial, 30; Markus Gebauer/Shutterstock Images, 33; LuAnne Cadd/Virunga National Park/AP Images, 34

CONTENTS

CHAPTER ONE

FOREST PROTECTORS

The tracker followed a narrow trail through an African forest. He scanned the dense undergrowth for snares, or traps. Poacher's snares were simple but deadly. A baby mountain gorilla had died recently after getting caught in a snare. The deep wounds in her leg became infected. The poachers were hunting for small antelope. But they often caught gorillas instead. The tracker did

Gorillas are super-smart animals that live across parts of Africa.

Snares

Poachers make snares using a piece of wire or rope. They shape the wire into a noose, or loop, and tie it to a flexible branch. They bend the branch until the noose lies flat on the ground. A rock holds the noose in place. Leaves are scattered on top to hide it. When an animal bumps the rock or pulls the rope, the branch springs back. The noose tightens around the animal and cuts into its flesh. Some gorillas can break the branch and get away. They cannot remove the noose, however. Many gorillas that escape from snares lose a hand or foot because the noose cuts off the blood supply to that limb.

not want that to happen again.

The tracker saw a snare. He moved closer to disable it. Suddenly a large adult male gorilla appeared out of the bushes. The gorilla grunted a warning. The tracker stopped and watched. Two young gorillas ran up to the snare. One jumped on the branch and broke it. The other yanked the wire noose out of the ground. They spotted another snare the tracker had not seen. A third young gorilla joined the group.

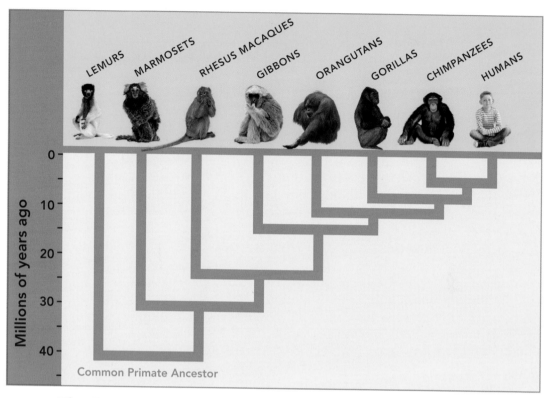

Millions of years ago

LEMURS MARMOSETS RHESUS MACAQUES GIBBONS ORANGUTANS GORILLAS CHIMPANZEES HUMANS

Common Primate Ancestor

The Primate Family Tree

Gorillas are one of the most closely related animals to humans. Gorillas and humans are both primates. This diagram shows the evolution of different primate species from a common ancestor and how long ago each animal split off as a separate species. After looking at this diagram, what do you think about the relationship between these two species? Are you surprised by how closely humans are related to gorillas? What other physical similarities can you see among the primate species?

Together they quickly tore apart the second snare.

The tracker was amazed. Scientists already knew adult

gorillas could find and break snares. But this was the

first time anyone had seen young gorillas outsmart

the poachers. The young gorillas had learned to work together to protect themselves.

Big Apes

Gorillas are members of a group of primates called apes. Apes have broad chests and arms that rotate easily. They do not have tails. Great apes are a group that includes gorillas, chimpanzees, orangutans, and humans.

Gorillas are divided into three subspecies based on where in Africa they live: eastern, western, and mountain gorilla.

Female gorillas can weigh up to 216 pounds (98 kg) and grow to almost 5 feet (1.5 m) tall. Adult male gorillas are up to two times heavier than females. An average male gorilla weighs 400 pounds (181 kg) and stands 5.6 feet (1.7 m) tall. Some gorillas in captivity can grow to more than 500 pounds (227 kg) and over 6 feet (1.8 m) tall. A gorilla's bulk makes it strong. Gorillas are up to six times stronger than humans.

A silverback gorilla does not have completely silver hair. The hair on the back and hips turns this color.

Gorillas are covered in thick black hair. Only their ears, lips, nose, palms, and the soles of their feet are hairless. Mountain gorillas have long hair that protects them from their cold and wet environment. Eastern gorillas have shorter, thicker hair than mountain gorillas. Western gorillas have short brown hair on their heads. Some male gorillas are called silverbacks. This is because the hair on their backs turns a silver-gray color when they take charge of a group. Gorillas have dark brown to black skin.

Gorilla Identification

Scientists tell gorillas apart by their noses. Each gorilla has a different pattern of wrinkles on the bridge of its nose. The nostrils can be oval or square. The fleshy part of the nose surrounding the nostrils, known as the nose wings, can be pointy or rounded. They can also have smooth or rough edges. Drawings or photos of gorilla noses are called nose prints. Each nose print is unique, just like human fingerprints.

Gorillas have huge shoulders, powerful arms, and enormous stomachs. Gorillas and humans have similar skeletons. Long arms allow gorillas to move on all four limbs. They walk on their knuckles with their fingers curled into a fist. Gorillas can also stand upright and walk for short distances. Opposable thumbs and big toes allow them to grip objects with their hands or feet.

A Gorilla's Head

Gorilla skulls are huge. Bony ridges on top of male gorilla skulls anchor the chewing muscles. These ridges make males' heads look like a cone. Powerful

Gorillas can see in color, which helps them spot food in a dark forest.

jaws help gorillas chew tough foods. They use their long, pointy teeth to scare away or bite rivals.

All gorillas have brown eyes. Gorillas have good eyesight. Both of their eyes face forward. Gorillas can see in three dimensions and estimate distances. Their strong eyesight helps them find their way through the forest and choose the best foods. Gorillas also have good hearing.

CHAPTER TWO

GORILLA LIFE

Gorillas live in family groups made up of 2 to 20 gorillas. Each group usually has one silverback, several adult females, and several infants. Sometimes large family groups with more than one silverback form. The silverback is the leader of the family. He settles arguments between family members and protects them from other gorillas.

Gorilla family groups vary in size. But all groups have a silverback as a leader.

Silverbacks have quick tempers. They are always on the lookout for danger, including another family group's silverback. Females often leave their own family groups to join another family. If two families cross paths and a female seems interested in joining the other family, the two families' silverbacks may fight one another.

Mating

A silverback mates with all of the adult females in his family group. A female gorilla gives birth to one baby at a time. Twins are very rare. After having a baby, it will be three to six years before a female gives birth again. If a new silverback takes over a family group, he may kill

Show of Strength

A silverback shows off when faced with danger. He hoots, roars, and screams. He bares his sharp teeth. The silverback may grab and throw plants. He runs around, stands up, and beats his chest. The loud drumming sound this makes can be heard from far away. The silverback may suddenly charge at his enemy. This display intimidates other silverbacks, scares away predators, and alerts family members. It also impresses female gorillas. It is a noisy, violent, and frightening show.

Although twin gorilla babies are rare, it does happen. These twins were born in a European zoo.

all the infants in the group. This makes the females more likely to mate again. The new silverback will then become a father himself.

A baby gorilla is tiny and helpless at birth. It weighs less than 5 pounds (2 kg). Babies are carried until they can hold onto their mothers' backs. Infants grow and develop quickly. They can walk and feed themselves at six months old. By four years old, gorillas weigh around 80 pounds (36 kg). Baby gorillas drink their mother's milk until they are three or four years old.

Moving On

Females leave their family group when they are between seven and ten years old. They usually join a new group of unrelated female gorillas. Male gorillas leave their family group when they are between nine and twelve years old. Males live alone or with other males until they become silverbacks and take over a group. Then they challenge older silverbacks to try to take over their families. The winner becomes the new leader of the group.

Instead of fighting, a young silverback may show off his strength to a family group. He tries to attract females to form a new family group with him. A female gorilla chooses the silverback she thinks will be the best leader and protector. Females often change family groups throughout their lifetimes.

Male gorillas often challenge each other. These challenges can turn into deadly fights.

A Day in a Gorilla's Life

Gorillas spend their time finding food, eating, and resting. Families wander freely through their home range. Gorillas eat leaves, fruit, stems, bark, and roots from many different plant species. Their diet depends on where they live. Lowland gorillas eat more fruit. Mountain gorillas like bamboo shoots. Gorillas near swamps munch the juicy roots of aquatic plants. Some gorillas also eat caterpillars, termites, ants, and grubs.

Gorillas use plants to make nests. They bend and weave branches into a large, comfortable place to sleep. They make new nests every day. Although adult male gorillas stay on the ground because of their size, lowland females and young gorillas make nests in trees.

Gorillas bond with family members by grooming one another. They comb through each other's hair and pick off ticks, lice, and other parasites using their fingers. They also remove scabs, dead skin, and dirt. Gorillas may clean wounds by licking them.

60-Pound Salad

Gorillas have big, round bellies. But they are not fat. They have large digestive systems. Gorillas eat more than any of the other apes. They have to eat large amounts of food to get the nutrients they need. Male gorillas can eat up to 60 pounds (27 kg) of food a day. Gorillas eat more than 100 different types of plants.

Wild gorillas live for approximately 30 to 40 years. When a silverback dies, another silverback may take over the family group. The family might also split up and join other groups or start new family groups.

CHAPTER THREE

MEASURING INTELLIGENCE

Scientists believe gorillas are very smart. A gorilla brain is approximately one-third the size of a human brain. Gorillas are thought to be smarter than monkeys but not as smart as humans.

Primatologists study gorilla behavior in the field. This gives them ideas about how gorillas think and learn. Captive gorillas can also be tested to study their intelligence.

Gorillas are intelligent creatures that have learned to solve problems in captivity and in the wild.

Mirror Test

When most animals look into mirrors, they treat their reflections like another animal. However, some gorillas and other apes recognize themselves in mirrors. Koko is a captive gorilla that lives in Maui, Hawaii. When Koko has a mirror placed in front of her, she makes faces and looks at her teeth. Koko understands the image in the mirror is her own face.

Using Tools

For a long time, scientists were not sure if wild gorillas used tools. Since it is easy for gorillas to find food, scientists believed these animals did not need tools. This thinking changed when researchers

Artistic Apes

Michael was a western lowland gorilla who lived with Koko. He learned American Sign Language (ASL). Michael also liked to paint. He used many different colors. One day Michael used only black and white paint. He named the painting "Apple Chase" by signing the words with his hands. But the picture did not look like an apple at all. His human friends realized Michael had painted his favorite activity, playing chase with a black and white dog. The dog's name was Apple!

A gorilla uses a stick to test the depth of swampy water before it crosses.

saw a female gorilla using a tool. She used a long stick to test how deep the water was in a pond. She crossed the pond by poking the stick into the water in front of her. Still, it is unusual for gorillas to make or use tools.

Gorilla Food Preparation

Nettle plants are covered with short hairs that cause a painful sting. But mountain gorillas love eating nettles anyway. They have learned how to avoid being stung. They strip leaves off the stalk and stack them up. Then they fold the stack of leaves over the stalks. This covers the stinging hairs inside. Now the gorillas can eat the nettles without stinging their mouths.

Mental Maps

Gorillas have very good memories. They remember where favorite nesting and feeding places are. Lowland gorillas return to certain areas when the fruit there is ripe. Some mountain gorillas head straight for the bamboo forests when bamboo shoots are beginning to grow. Gorillas also go back to a place months after feeding there so they can eat the tender new leaves that have grown.

Communication

Gorillas also prove their intelligence by their ability to communicate with each other and with humans. Koko's caregivers have been teaching her American Sign Language (ASL) since she was a baby. Now she uses over 1,000 ASL words. She understands some English words too. Koko has conversations with people using sign language. She also makes up her own signs for objects. Koko can even read some printed words. When Koko took Intelligence Quotient (IQ) tests, she scored as well as a four- to five-year-old human.

Other gorillas besides Koko communicate among themselves. Mountain gorillas have more than 22 different sounds they make with their voices. Gorillas also use their hands to communicate. One group of zoo gorillas uses more than 40 gestures.

Koko learned to use sign language to communicate with humans when she was one year old.

Emotions

Gorillas show fear, anger, affection, happiness, and sadness. They even have a sense of humor. Koko likes to scare her human friends with her toy alligator. She makes jokes and laughs at silly things. For many years, Koko had a pet cat named All Ball. When Koko's cat died, she was very sad and made noises that sounded like crying. Koko also seems to have empathy. This is the ability to feel sad for other people or animals.

Dr. Penny Patterson taught Koko ASL for nine years. In a book she wrote about this experience, she talks about why it is hard to answer questions about Koko's intelligence:

> The answer would seem to be a simple problem of administering intelligence tests. Determining Koko's IQ, however, is not so simple, for a variety of reasons having to do with the nature of the subject, the nature of intelligence tests, and . . . the nature of intelligence itself. . . .
>
> Answers that seem perfectly plausible to a gorilla must sometimes be scored as errors on standardized tests. For instance . . . one question directs . . . "Point to the two things that are good to eat." The choices are a block, an apple, a shoe, a flower, and an ice-cream sundae. Koko picked the apple and the flower. Another question asked. . . where. . . to shelter from the rain. The choices were a hat, a spoon, a tree, and a house. Koko . . . chose the tree.

Source: Francine Patterson and Eugene Linden. *The Education of Koko.* New York: Holt, Rinehart and Winston, 1981. Print. 124.

Back It Up

Dr. Patterson is using evidence to support her point. Write a paragraph describing the point she is making. Then write down one or two pieces of evidence Patterson uses to make her point.

CHAPTER FOUR

HABITAT AND THREATS

Gorillas live in African rain forests near the equator. Western lowland gorillas have the largest range. Mountain gorillas have the smallest range. The lowland forests eastern and western gorillas call home are hot and humid. Mountain forests are cool and misty.

Approximately 8,000 different species of plants grow in the rain forest. These plants supply food and

Among gorilla species, Western lowland gorillas roam the largest area of Africa.

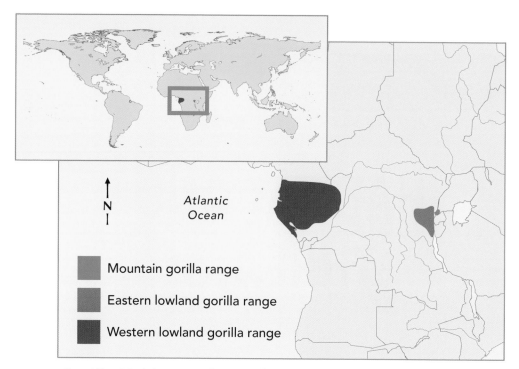

Gorilla Habitat and Population Map

This map shows the habitat range of gorillas. Gorillas live in rain forests in Africa. What characteristics make gorillas well adapted to this type of habitat? Use information from this chapter to back up your ideas.

shelter. The forests are so dense that a 500-pound (227-kg) gorilla can easily hide there. Gorillas do not have to travel far to get a meal. They are surrounded by food.

Predators

Gorillas are strong and fierce. They do not have many natural predators. Some scientists believe leopards prey on gorillas. But the biggest threat to their survival is humans.

It is illegal to hunt or trap gorillas. But the countries where gorillas live do not always enforce these laws. Gorilla hunters and poachers often go unpunished. Some use gorilla heads and hands to make trophies and souvenirs. Some African healers use gorilla skulls and other body parts in their rituals. Gorilla meat is sold as food for humans. Snares kill or cripple gorillas. Some baby gorillas are sold as pets when they are captured alive. Most baby gorillas do not survive as pets for long.

Human Wars

When humans in Africa fight each other, gorillas suffer. Long civil wars in central Africa have caused the deaths of many gorillas. Some soldiers camp in the forests. They kill gorillas for meat. They sometimes kill scientists too. Other scientists have been forced to abandon their research and flee areas where fighting is happening. The governments are too busy fighting to protect the gorillas.

Threats to Gorillas

The biggest threat to gorillas is the destruction of their habitats. All across Africa, people are cutting down forests. Trees are used for lumber or charcoal. The land is turned into farms and ranches. Minerals are mined from newly deforested areas.

As people clear the forests, animals are forced to live in smaller areas. This also brings people closer to the gorillas. Human diseases such as the Ebola virus can spread to gorillas. This deadly virus killed 5,000 western lowland gorillas in 2006 alone. There is no cure for Ebola.

Gorilla Doctors

Some mountain gorillas get a checkup once a month. The veterinarians of the Mountain Gorilla Veterinary Project make house calls. They hike into the forest and observe each gorilla for signs of illness or injury. They give the gorillas vaccines and medicines using dart guns. They sometimes give sleeping drugs to gorillas caught in snares or with open wounds. This allows the vets to get close enough to the animals to cut the snare off or stitch up wounds.

Human activities, such as logging, are threatening gorillas' homes and survival rates.

National parks and sanctuaries in Africa are doing all they can to protect gorillas from disease and poachers.

Gorillas are on the edge of extinction. They are an endangered species. Western and mountain gorillas are critically endangered. Scientists fear that within 10 to 15 years, there will be no more gorillas in the wild. Many conservation groups are working to save the ones that are left. Patrols guard the parks where gorillas live to protect the animals from poachers. Veterinarians treat sick gorillas. Sanctuaries take in orphaned gorillas. But civil wars in some African

FURTHER EVIDENCE

There is quite a bit of information about threats to gorilla habitats in Chapter Four. What is the main point of this chapter? What evidence is given to support this point? Go to the Web site at the link below. Find a quote on this Web site that supports the main point of this chapter. Does the quote support an existing piece of evidence in the chapter? Or does it add a new one? Write a few sentences explaining how the quote you found relates to this chapter.

Gorilla Rescue
www.mycorelibrary.com/gorillas

countries have put conservation workers in danger.

Until these countries become more stable, the future

of gorillas will be uncertain.

CHAPTER FIVE

THE IMPORTANCE OF GORILLAS

G orillas and humans have a lot in common. We share 97.7 percent of our genes with gorillas. Only chimpanzees are more closely related to humans.

An Important Species

Gorillas are an important part of the forest ecosystem. When gorillas eat, they trim plants. This encourages the plants to grow. Gorillas also spread seeds to

It is important for humans to take better care of gorillas so they do not become extinct.

The Problem with Tourism

Some gorillas are used to being watched by people. For a fee, tourists who come to Africa can visit gorillas. The money helps pay for gorilla care, protection, and research. The tours also create jobs for villagers living near the gorillas' habitat. But there are problems with tourism too. Visitors carry diseases. And gorillas that are used to people do not run from poachers. Conservation groups are worried this type of tourism may harm gorillas more than it helps them. Tourists must now stay at a distance and can observe gorillas for only one hour at a time.

different parts of the forest. They affect the kind of plants that make up the forest.

The health of the forests and the gorillas are linked. To prevent the extinction of gorillas, humans must stop cutting down the forests. Saving the forests will help save gorillas and other endangered animals.

Scientists are interested in learning more about ape intelligence. Over the years, groups of scientists used special machines to scan human and gorilla

Researchers and scientists continue to learn more about gorillas as they spend more time with them.

brains. The scans took videos of brain activity. The patients were awake but resting. The results showed the language centers of the human brains were active. The same scans showed different parts of the gorillas' brains were active. Since gorillas do not use words, they most likely think in a different way than humans.

Ozzie, the Oldest Gorilla

Gorillas in zoos live longer than wild gorillas. Ozzie is the world's oldest living male zoo gorilla. When he turned 52 on April 24, 2013, Ozzie's home, Zoo Atlanta in Georgia, threw him a big birthday party. Ozzie communicates with his keepers with sounds and by knocking on windows. Ozzie is famous for being the first gorilla to have his blood pressure measured. An extra-large, extra-strong inflatable cuff was made to fit the 350-pound (159-kg) gorilla.

Although different parts of their brains are active, these studies show a gorilla's brain is more similar to a human brain than previously believed.

Gorilla research helps scientists answer questions about these intelligent animals. Gorillas continue to be threatened by human activity. It is important for humans to help conserve gorilla habitats. Then these super-smart animals will be around for many more years.

Paola Cavalieri and Peter Singer's book *The Great Ape Project* discusses the need for people to treat apes as equals because of their intelligence. The following excerpt comes from an essay in the book called "A Declaration on Great Apes":

> [In] "the community of equals" . . . we accept certain basic . . . rights . . . Among these . . . rights are . . . the Right to Life; the Protection of Individual Liberty; The Prohibition of Torture.
>
> At present, only members of the species Homo sapiens are regarded as members of the community of equals. . . . The chimpanzee, the gorilla and the orangutan are the closest relatives of our species. They also have mental capacities and an emotional life sufficient to justify inclusion within the community of equals.
>
> Source: Paola Cavalieri and Peter Singer. The Great Ape Project: Equality Beyond Humanity. New York, St. Martin's Press, 1993. Print. 4–5.

Changing Minds

Do you think gorillas should have the same rights as humans, as discussed in the excerpt? Imagine that your best friend has the opposite position. Write a brief essay trying to change your friend's mind. Make sure you explain your opinion and your reasons for it. Include facts and details that support your reasons.

Common Name: Gorilla

Scientific Name: *Gorilla gorilla*

Average Size: 5.6 feet (1.7 m) tall for adult males; 4.9 feet (1.5 m) tall for adult females

Average Weight: Up to 400 pounds (181 kg) for adult males; up to 216 pounds (98 kg) for adult females

Color: Mostly black; as they get older, some males have silver hair on their backs

Average Lifespan: 35 years in the wild; 50 years in captivity

Diet: Leaves, bark, stems, flowers, and fruit of many different plant species; gorillas also eat ants, termites, caterpillars, and grubs

Habitat: The thick, humid rain forests of Africa, near the equator

Threats: Humans and leopards

Intelligence Features

- Captive gorillas can be taught to use American Sign Language and understand some spoken English.
- Gorillas are able to create, follow, and repeat a series of actions in a specific sequence.
- Gorillas are able to solve problems.

Another View

This book has a lot of information about gorilla intelligence. As you know, every source is different. Ask a librarian or another adult to help you find a reliable source about animal intelligence. Write a short essay comparing and contrasting the new source's point of view with that of this book's author. What is the point of view of each author? How are they similar and why? How are they different and why?

Take a Stand

This book discusses how hunters set snares and sometimes catch gorillas accidentally. Take a position on poachers setting snares in gorilla territories. Write a short essay explaining your opinion. Make sure to give reasons for your opinion. Give some evidence to support your reasons.

Surprise Me

Learning about gorillas can be interesting and surprising. Think about what you learned from this book. Can you name two or three facts about gorillas you found surprising? Write a short paragraph about each fact. Why did you find them surprising?

Tell the Tale

Chapter Four discusses how people are cutting down African forests. Write 200 words about logging activities. Describe the sights and sounds gorillas might see or hear. What can the gorillas do to protect themselves? Be sure to set the scene, develop a sequence of events, and offer a conclusion.

GLOSSARY

ancestor
individuals or species that
lived a long time ago

captivity
confined without an escape

conservation
careful preservation and
protection of something

disease
a specific illness

lowland
low and usually level ground

mineral
a naturally occurring
substance

opposable
capable of being placed
against one or more fingers
or toes

predator
an animal that kills and eats
other animals

primatologist
a scientist who studies
primates

poacher
someone who hunts or fishes
unlawfully

rain forest
a tropical forest where a lot
of rain falls

LEARN MORE

Books

Sobol, Richard. *Breakfast in the Rain Forest: A Visit with Mountain Gorillas.* Somerville, MA: Candlewick, 2008.

Turner, Pamela S. *Gorilla Doctors.* Boston: Houghton Mifflin, 2008.

Zobel, Derek. *Gorillas.* Minneapolis: Bellwether Media, 2012.

Web Links

To learn more about gorillas, visit ABDO Publishing Company online at **www.abdopublishing.com**. Web sites about gorillas are featured on our Book Links page. These links are routinely monitored and updated to provide the most current information available.

Visit **www.mycorelibrary.com** for free additional tools for teachers and students.

INDEX

ABOUT THE AUTHOR

Before becoming an author, Andrea Wang worked as an environmental scientist and helped clean up hazardous waste sites. She gets the shivers when she looks into a gorilla's intelligent brown eyes.